BUT NOW

BUT NOW

Phyllis Perlstone

PUNCHER & WATTMANN

First published in 2022
Published by Puncher and Wattmann
PO Box 279
Waratah NSW 2298

https://www.puncherandwattmann.com
web@puncherandwattmann.com

ISBN   9781922571434

Cover design by David Musgrave, from a drawing by Phyllis Perlstone
Typesetting by Morgan Arnett
Printed by Lightning Source International

NATIONAL
LIBRARY
OF AUSTRALIA

A catalogue record for this work is available from the National Library of Australia

For Alwyn   1930–2020

on first hearing how long

I Would Have Shown You This If There Was Time

She clasped and unclasped her hands
drawing her fingers together
and loosening them
like a car weaving in and out of lanes
trying to reach the other side of the traffic
to turn
to turn her thoughts over
all the while staring through a window
on to a city scene   cluttered with buildings
and streets   laid out like a frantic power board
now caught static in a winter sun
not strong enough to keep everything in motion
always

Contents

Portraits: Points of Viewing

The Seasons Where You Are

Constructing a City

Politics and Anxiety

Preface

I started this series of poems with writing one of them after a visit to Byron Bay then a few more about the beach there and its incredible beauty. My first memories about beauty and freedom (which seemed the same thing) come from when my childhood was sporadically lifted from what I felt was Sydney suburban dullness or confinement as well as boredom. Rescue and excitement were in weekend ferry trips to Nielsen Park and its beach.

The house we lived in was on South Street which was on a border between Marrickville and Dulwich Hill. I think my infants and kindergarten schools were in Marrickville and my primary school in Dulwich Hill. There was family strife and upset later, when in the middle of the second world war in 1943/44 we were evicted from this ordinary existence – 'ordinary' except for a couple of upheavals when my mother was very ill in the Great Depression and again when my sisters were born three and four years apart and my father couldn't look after my brother and me. My other early memories were of being in a couple of 'Homes'. One was easy-going since it was a Convalescent Home for adults who were amused by us – though it was terribly different from being at home. The other was regimented and strange. It was an orphanage.

All this while my father was working in a factory – the only job he could get after the depression during which he and his father sold fish (door-to-door) which they managed to buy at the fish markets. His early working hours started for him at 4 or 5 in the morning when he would to rise to make my mother a cup of tea, which helped to set her up for her day, now four children and much house work, etc. Then he would go on to catch a tram to Broadway, where the factory was, to start work about maybe an hour later.

Writing this now, I realise just how hard it was for my father. He didn't mind, I think, when we were in our Marrickville house where my mother felt lucky and pretty happy to be. My father changed after we were evicted. He turned into someone who at times could hardly be anything other than raving and incoherent. My mother became depressed and unable to look forward in any way. My father and his father, my mother and we four children lived in a terrace slum (actually 'condemned') in Alexandria. The Marrickville house had been adequate for all of us but not this house, where my grandfather was left with a room that doubled as a laundry and was the only passage to the toilet outside.

A cultural division started between my mother – the daughter of somewhat Orthodox Judaism – and my grandfather whose Judaism was strictly orthodox, something that was impossible to maintain in our domestically confined life. This division my father watched and was torn by and we children including my brother (going through adolescence) all watched pretty helplessly, feeling our distance too, wondering at the hard feelings.

"The Hungry Mile" (where I now live) – now Barangaroo – is a frame for most of the poems in BUT NOW: they cover life in our city, as the hard history of a certain part of it, set against an intermittent desire to get away from the discontents of its civilisation, towards the beauty of its shores and trees.

Prologue

All I Imagine

as I subject my poems   or my purposes
to whatever I can make out

not wanting to have been careless
worse to have meant to be

care now is harder
for having even less efficacy

wanting to say
no measure

for any measure
is enough

beseeching
time

Portraits: Points of Viewing

Celebrate

The simulacrum
of a photograph
fills with our feelings

after all you just have to see
by this harbour
       where you hold a breath at the sea's rush
       under the silver banksias
       rattling quietly the cool air of the morning
you are walking through
like someone unencumbered

~

The day was bright
the house in the garden sun had shade
the bric-a-brac dark of extending boughs
easier to see in   to greet each face

the break in the trees
blinded us with dazzle
light at the entrance   before
we stood inside

the ferns were a ceremony
the grey spotted plants arcing
curved downwards
hiding a solitude

for the guests coming in
it was a time to alleviate feeling
now you see you regard some with deep hurts
their shock

~

And then it's Mahler's song 'I'm lost to the world'
the piano's a stream for the voice
dipping in to words
their thoughts

the sounds grow apart   the singer
has lengthened them   stretched the nothing but air
for music's
rhapsody of containment

~

the day cooling
the grass still soft
after cakes and wine
everyone steps   further

goes on
like sunset's closing light
celebration stops and whatever is private
returns to inhabit us

the familiar   or old re-starts   wobble
us   as if being away
and then being back
we are   in 'tinier circles'

~

Yet it's not the leaning plants
nor the music
not the sea ruffling
by the harbour

not water slipping in and out
from a wake
splashing white on a piece of pumice
a small pebble   fixed yet loose in it   that swivels

if you now understand
though you couldn't once
it is as if whatever the edges were
the past   turns you

What You Take for Granted

They look like
your memory of them
portray those you love
a smile in black and white looks silvery
screened light is diamond pointed

then the white and black grades grey
the present charges the words of once-were

to go from then to not knowing enough

having only a space to look across

blank unbridged   or water
    the same as air
you put a hand in
and never touch a thing
except your own thinking

still in that photograph you see
more of time spent   from the snapped-off photo
in the 1930s   when they walk on
on a day out
before a return to much
they have to laugh away

this as if
your mother and her sister should continue
in their unbroken dream

the image   was what they aspired to
the clothes they wore
the jazzy brightness of a movie star
they could pretend
to a comedienne-mockery of things

you knew in their quick-silvery pictures
fast back-tracking
before you —
how though they couldn't better
film's purer romance
of flaws as foibles only
against their later realness —
their caught smiles
keep the photo clear

At Observatory Park

for A.L.K.

It's complicated
the delay is in the long unravelling
when eyes   not resolving
the tiny residue
of ourselves —
see only
a landscape-scene-photo

in the distance

up and across the harbour   white sky   sea mist
trees in a line
with a dot of red
and something else

It's your dog   a brown figurine
and the red is your dress (more ceramic)
by chance you're in the shot   as in the movie "Blow Up"

I've taken an incident   not of a crime scene
only the evidence   of seeing things   not meant to be familiar

now
I recognise you
unfolding from a stranger
sprung   vivid   as I know you
on my stand-still eyes

Visiting You in Brisbane

for M.K.

Gold scroll of beach   cloud like drifting steam across the sea
                     a head-tilted flight attendant pours drinks
                  moves glasses from tray to tray
                     balancing them slowly
                        as if machine-lifting larger things

the News in the video above   the orthodoxy
of a judge in his wig

a pocket window on a river beneath
brings distance close
cuts a running film
presages a narrative on the land

ranges are brain-like folds
the crinkled edgings and the vastness
going to whatever is furthest
describe our unnaturalness

as speed streams the way
we have ourselves

the plane going into land
estranges us   rising and falling

first a circle around
till we're out of flying
then the laid-out Brisbane towers
stand up against the sea

roofs   mass past
some homes on a hill

and mind slips
from the white sky and coast

into a hotel of old marble rooms
where lights
digitally change   colours startle
vision bounces in the room

2.
you phone –
my edged noticing
ceases
your voice sounds freely against it

you're close again –
your home so bird-and-tree decorated
the steps up to it
and seeing you at first this time

it's fast then it's slowly I take in
changes children surround you
with   likely more to come after your last
news   we don't have enough time

I now though
        as I see you with your loves
past 'Facebook'
on from videos' delight   too

though moving – they catch still
only at the vanishing
Yet you   and all of you   now I'm here
resume what voices and faces do

Self-Portrait

To watch carefulness in yourself   is it to think
that it's like a line around a space
of trying to see
consequences

Knowing there are tensions   I think of how
Matisse has drawn himself with hatted ears
he thickens the join of lines looped to each other
with studs of ink   mimicking a cell's division
the pressing and pulling away
the drawing running on   – enclosing –
to make the ellipse
the image of his face

What draws you
You can't run in one line
yet spinning
on a point
you loved being at
suddenly
you're not on that spot
after all   you're not where you were

Another likeness composed
might open on a new plane
where your care of whatever seemed
bounded was an irritant
or like fire   red   then oxygen-less
charcoaled later into how you see
the only visual remnant
of dying numbers of yourself

A foghorn sounds across the harbour
the noise of cars below the window
the little light below the small
lifting of the blind
brings morning and new consequences
with a longer background
as you
remember

It's not as if impulse is freed
inhibition lies in your decisions
or in awry cracks
in reasons

New electronic tracking
sees
what you will do
before you're consciously

intent
shows up in scans
on glassy screens
as your line shifts

Pixels dot you over too
doing and undoing
you standing still
you're in the spot
you wanted to rub away —
do snap-shots show you looking harder
as if to brook what is —
you can't see

Self-portraits flutter and fail
their reconnaissance of you
with or without you wanting
other eyes engaging
with or without love
through their lens
depict you
sometimes as a stranger —

the stranger-you
interrogates
or smiling   puts a hat on
or dark glasses

To Draw Like That

squash pigment
wet on rock   or finger it   or use a stick

from memory

        the moment   recalled
          many times
of an echidna seen

someone 1700 years ago
records that   achieves a likeness
the thing so much in mind
has put it down

Smiling and Talks of Change   Maybe Dancing?

1.

Dusk at the airport looking to New York's towers
    the 'high-rise' sky
columns   like memorials keeping their heads
above the horizon   in an orange sky the black buildings
flattening in travel's comical distance
change to a stencilled delicate design
industry's planting for gardenless rooms

2.

Carved and cubed in morning light
old buildings elaborate on the new plainness
then in the sunset pink
our hotel's rooftop garden
looks on to gold-plated windows
New York in O'Keefe's desert colours

we're gazing with out-of-town Americans
("here for the tennis 'Open'")
the spreading rose
tinges a towerless horizon
the day too summery hot to gather thoughts
Yet in the hotel we remember

our friend's beautiful blue shirt   as he guided us
to the city's Gardens   in strong sun he showed us
contrasts   how we are in the city
Big strides of wide streets   trees sometimes
sometimes concrete only
New York mythic   'real'

He showed us antiques
he'd brought home
from Australia
put them on carpets with the cat
who posed
in the centred swirls

3.
Yet we've come this day from the Guggenheim
we saw Saddam Hussein's face doubly exposed
chaos's art form   negative and dark printed
the pre-emptive lip   the traced eyes like light
around and underlining
emptiness too   the artist will not let him go
but preserves the dead dictator's
lack
the affectless
riddle
we might have forgotten
the look of autocracy's features

4.
Our friend had decided   his world
home's hard power   'the 70's' darkening
him   to travel from America to Australia
then after years he's home again
America's in 'new' old wars
in 'not-so-queasy' destruction now

His loved sister
last of his family
the close one   had died —
from that recoil
to reach to see
past all that is not your own

5.

In a blue shirt today   a fine blue   he looks out
and smiles
here in the Botanical Gardens in New York
he's not letting go
not for abjection   not for its sake
he keeps friendship's warmth

He made the drive smooth
one hand on the wheel   two hands and we all
looked at the view   the Hudson's slow motion
passes trees
as they disappear   no cover for sorrow —

Yet to remember with him in Australia
meals   talking   his first sighting of 'our
world'   likenesses to less
of the worst he saw   we didn't always —
our puzzle —
his praise sometimes a wonder to us

Now   in this new grief
in America   home flashed
too short a light
on 'his little cloud'

though we catch at his hurt's strain
he didn't try to speak of it

6.
Today in the bright unshadowed
spaces we toured —
the gardens' waterlilies on a lake
are like hands spreading fingers
around the leaves   dispersing
the colours they hold together

his wife smiling says
"Maybe we'll go dancing?
We used to"

Away from the City

for S.B.

Car-tyres hose the roads   their numbers take up time
truck wheels mean to overturn the past
make the present longer lasting
dig hills to flatness
straightening direction to future's speed

and harbour water
still running   racing with itself
only the city
limits

from all this you wanted to be away
you kept saying
you could look all day
at the hairline wisp-young
trees   wild
branch and leaf
you could resolve distances
even as uncontained
shapes
imperceptible
except for the earth
stretching
to include them
you could look
close-up
see a flower-spraying bush
frail
in its star-like growth

among the vastness
of others
intricate
in its slightness
breezing colours
into

whether they are noticed
or not

Not Yet My Oblivion

for A.J.K.

From years ago
relative to this void now
oblivion is for the one dying

none for the living —
remembering and remembering
the void now

Is it a history truly then
of the generations interrupting
not us puncturing

you could laugh
shaking happiness out of
very small delights

a child or a funny thing —
I don't deny the wry too
in you

that when we're older nothing's
as easy
getting more difficult quickly

no summing up —
my understanding only discriminates
now what ends with your going

It's a mixture still
glad of the long-lasting
affecting me

remembering those
promontories of time

The Seasons Where You Are

Grey and Winter Sometimes

Grey and winter sometimes childhood
the wind then like boredom
colourless within walls
always   no change
no shadows or sun but
sun would tell me
what was harsh around
except what was around
changed in summer
sometimes   father   mother
had ideas and things moved

My Father I Remember

He could look pleased
and be just as wordless

What   what if he'd had another life
not working in a factory

standing all day getting
varicose veins in his legs

My father's words?
they were shouts

The 'particulars' then of my father's house
a tenement of glassless walls

Yet now we find ourselves   where we live in the city
Barangaroo   in see-through heights   aspirations

                ..   ..   ..

Like a thought through water
in that water falling

over the nails of my fingers
in iridescence on the sand

searching for shells
a piece drifting under the sea

slipping slowly till it ran faster
evanescent in a pull-away wave —

it was my father invented for us
these sweet beach days

                .. .. ..

I try to see him
the clues   the definiens

My father in an old photo
held a cigarette with stiff fingers

he'd drink only Shabbos wine
on high-holy days like his father

Was he mates with the other workers
was it words then for silently labouring

he didn't want to find   to unlock his tongue
from the rest of his body   sealed to silver-

plating spoons   in the machines
muting him   multiply producing   shining sets

all his puzzled standing-hours
the Company could hold him

Raging hungry   home from the factory
he looked his plight

back with us he was our ogre
my mother hurried with the meat

                ..   ..   ..

He'd lent money
to a broke work mate

poorer than him   he said —
living in a housing commission home

When my younger sisters were sick
he bought them delicate fish

                ..   ..   ..

He read romantic novels when he was younger
by Georgette Heyer   later it was J.B. Priestley

and A.J. Cronin   he wouldn't share with us
what they mirrored for him

whatever he stared at through them
what it was to assemble   pieces

read-through   as if *there*
with others he was recognisable

What he knew in
'those times'

'Nothing in it' for my mother
after the eviction from the 'other' house

solitary   dream-deprived
her "part" removed

the play-out she'd hoped for
in watching over us

cutting the cloth of it
she had cut away all

till she could not choose
kind and colour in most things

Stored in a drawer   white lace   maroon velvet —
the curtains bought before   "I won't hang them 'here' "

                    ..   ..   ..

Swimming is for the speechless
(drowning too — your mouth full of not saying)

At dawn on his holidays my father
though older   would walk

early   as on a work day
from Alexandria to Coogee

walk into the beachwater
throwing it onto him

bend and slide into the wet and slope
immerse in sea look at sky

water-weighed   seeing
more than the land-stopped

the lit-and-leave-you
transparency moving

in all-day light
My father's eyes were already blue

an immigrant from England
with his (Yiddish-speaking)

father and mother (she soon to die)
they'd already taken themselves from Poland —

my father knew summer now
in this country

Though it is the fixity of the city holds me
in rough weather

            ..   ..   ..

In the Town Hall   Sydney
my father took me to hear Yasha Heifitz

or was it Isaac Stern playing?
I listened   for him

the strings' high pitch threw
pure sound's puzzle into that time

He took me also to his factory near Broadway
down the lane

the smell of chickens
I saw women plucking them in a doorway

.. .. ..

Running to meet you Dad after work
the tram stop at the top of the street

When was that
before the eviction

Later-on   after the eviction
my mother said   'hide that we live here'

There were two houses
I remember front and back

green   and no green
one serene   one a racket

two fathers
one alive and one a falling stone

But wait   my father his purpose
to keep going   the rising day

not letting go the sense
that his city fixed him in

till some un-sensing in him prevailed
as if habit only had held his head

not his words   not in his words

Coastal: a Diary

We look for trees —
in heat small figs are no canopy —
The breeze the sea sends
while gazing at water
I try to think this is shaded
at the edge where waves finally
hit
and river cats and cruisers
and ferries hurry past

the footing in this park —
the flatness breaks —
flakes of stone
and rounded pebbles
in the way
though suddenly the blue is harbouring us
in the high leaf dark of trees

The punctuation marks
of sea-craft crossing the water
slow down my thoughts
rising with morning's
memory of
my father's words

It is still enough here
the bands of sky   water
and land   lying over each other
are like things placed to settle

.. .. ..

Meandering mind   catches
misses
the instances
but it's recursive —
the day comes back
to what had not been said

I watch the waterline
my mind's not oceanic
but particular
loving that high crane there
sloping   through
the flat
continuous distance

.. .. ..

The sun shines through green transparencies
x-rays of light among trees' shadows
loops and flares of leaves
fringed plants so delicate
the different breezes
swing them
like expectancies not counted on
to sway the mind

Elaborate riffs of a bird you can't see
the air gets struck with its chords
a currawong swoops in a warble
its flash its sound goes

like the absence
the pause
is more silent
than not expecting the trees
to hide anything

         ..   ..   ..

When we walk against the surf
when we fit our shoed feet
over prints
on claws of a bird
the paw of a dog
over rings of a sneaker
on toes of bare feet
the sand is white as paper

Out in the surf today
it's rough there's a rip
there's no quiet part
sitting in the sun
I'm burning

my hat blows off
the wind forcing waves about
new surfers going out to catch
waves stronger than they are
they're
back   dripping
the sea's so long
larger and higher
they run into it again
press a path

like running a thread under and over linen
pushing through a fold with a narrow needle
that bends   it would hurt if it broke

the water breaks
its weight a smothering cloth
the fear of drowning
is of being speechless

                 ..   ..   ..

Back in the city
why should I want anything wilder
the sea is full of rain
pigeons
whirr between two buildings
in rain-flouting grey they buzz
at corners   angles   straight lines –
unwinding to their roosts
water drops feather them
they shake out the glitter

buildings edging to the sea
stain
rain rides in thickening
surf foams on the beach
washes back shallow
white
over under-the-sea stones
and shore drifting animals
shells of others fling
into sand's gritting rush

gulls fly into the city
they swim the traffic

.. .. ..

Cool breezes and leaves
a chemical-carrying ship
comes between all of Goat Island
and this headland
grey
against the figs' green

a wall moving
filling the harbour
I hear gulls mewing
I can't see them
dotting the water
in their white-stopped crowds

.. .. ..

I listen to the sound in Barangaroo
of a noisy miner
under a shade tree
while the wake of the ship
presses out waves
in low-tide neatness

The harbour buildings are quiet
yet they take up sky
leave the park only half
in solitude
the city in these reaches

clears to a world that's thickest
in stone

if more stone is a thing
we don't mind their rocking
these frothy consequences
on white   soft   shores

will there be enough
trees and birds
we to walk under them
with the other wingless

         ..   ..   ..

North the long coast and a beach straight-lining —
along it the sea   blue ocean water
like a boulder tumbling till it falls
furls   top-heavy
rolls over under itself

It's as if Sisyphus
has stopped here on the beach
gathering the sea instead of stones
to climb with the water repeatedly
his emotions too hard
to contain
endlessly undoing and tightening
around his regret that nothing can be let go

Yet the sea is in sun and the sand is thickly
stepped-on
see the jumping water

and the yellow shore
transfigure us with their brightness

as we for ourselves
figure on these things   separately

The Unsafe World

for Pam M.

a sky writer
can't bat away any noise
of what's below
this protest in cursive smoke
the thin white he's spelling out
on a blue-plate
is spilling cloud like milk
blurring words

sitting in the balcony's sun
watching that poured whiteness
fall un-cupped
I imagine the showman's wings
dip as if to hit
not sky
but a bird
flying

when we were sitting in the sun
outside a café
talking
despite the braking and pushing cars
the buses bulking at their terminus
the tourist ones with people gazing

we still   then
side by side

in sun on a bench
could draw
the thinking-of-things-to-ourselves
into thinking-out-loud
hear ourselves say
the great day
though it trailed its curled ribbons
its invisible DNA around itself
was   almost   only   beautiful

Winter

In plain air
the surround-sound
of birds
is loud
they're invisible

then crowds
horizons of cloud
white breaths
of what's possible

cockatoos' wings
move the wind

out of trees
in black flight
distant
their shrieking directions
catch us
shouting

Yellow

on deciduous trees

wind by the sea's
on my face

the dangling discs
on branches
are like sun
in the
cold

Premonitions

like the updraft of a fire   the wind is vertiginous
pulls us to the sea's closeness
its taste is smelt in blue peaking tips

an afternoon sun at 4 o'clock sharpens the glitter
till there's nothing that looking at doesn't blind −

inferences of ends make brilliance   all dazzle
like starriness complete

Expectation

Looking back from the veranda
when the heat a door opens on is a fire
you smell air's eucalyptus burning
you're pulled back inside

a memory stronger than time
you inhale coming and going
from the sea to the city
it's not in anger   but helplessness
everyday
to construct another meaning
to turn to

The Gorgeous Red

of a bushfire
on the tv screen

a whole pizza oven
of flame

it's sunset in our living room
turning a sea yellow outside

as we watch the tv news
of the sky   over
the man and woman   picking through
the buckled   hooped iron roofs

lying on the ground   smoke wriggling
from the charred pieces —

here with us there's a ferry
crossing over the grey and yellow sea

veils of smoke
deep layers on the city

and trees behind them —
we're tired of the veils' mystery

the air is smoke
not mirrors twinning beauty

To Darwin and the Kimberley

1. Getting there

Above the brown cracked flat
there's a white furze on blue space
the window's pin-hole lens telescopes out
in sun on land long as a movie
running on over stretching scenes
a surprise in the film's
opening shots

if those slits are water
or clefts in ground darkened
between dry banks

this plane sidling
to the left and straightening
to Darwin
portends
heat and strangeness

2. Photo — bus trip out of Darwin

Dwindled to a Giacometti spindle in the landscape
a figure looking at a memorial in the sun's
shadow   is stalling

the Stuart Highway's on a name plate
in brass on a mound   some trees behind him
history he should know   or the delicate poles

of young eucalypts   branches splaying into crowds
of leaves   a tessellated mass   no glitter through it
the dark trunks stop him   sculpted as he is

shadows labour over his head
Should he move into the sun's heat
then walk on gravelled ground

bleach-eyed   go further
inspect war's artefacts
in the shed museum

pay tribute to these
when so much is gone of once unwithered trees
their leaves' long hanging shade

or should he only say
this happened
letting go history

3. In the Kimberley

An egret points its beak along the estuary
stares towards the fixity of the shore's
long rounding-off of lines

the bird is white-still
only its shadow on the water
shakes

it lifts
moon-coloured
where everything is blue or green

and hangs legs folded
under a trapeze of its wings

sky-art before it's disassembled

4. On Jar Island

Another egret is a curve over ground
stretching neck and beak like a string

putting its toes down considering
whether there's a flick or a wriggle

in the grit   the mud between
its wide apart walk

outside our boat
our shadows dangle

they screen our shapes into stretching forms
playing on water

the egret lifts
rows the air with sudden wings

our eyes in their glaze look down
to the bright green running under us

5. A Grey Egret

on the reef its neck an 's'
the head erect
surfaces
against grey mud
drawing
        its foot
aligning wing to tail
this egret is small   peaking and dropping
at the edge of the water   its eye onto
an appearance of something
loses it yet stays   stalks forward
pointing
        lingers again

        leaves

mends the crack in the sky

6. A crocodile

all mouth
and tail and scale
eye
and open jaw
suns on mud
along its back all spine   articulate craquelure −
imagine touching it
or watch its heavy tail
heave and twist and body-thick
    slide

just a body landed for blood

I'm thinking that it will be quick
its weight zig-zagging
like an arrow faster
than the thought of it
turning in front of me

7. *Welcome to Country*

Neville, oldest of the three   obliges
lends himself to be taken
yet leans away from the camera

unsure I press the button quickly
on him   Natalie a story-teller   and Kerry-Ann
an artist

who waits ochre-fingered ready
to paint a spot on our faces
smudges us with yellow

we're wet-earth gritted   solemn
polite   this touch on our skin
dips us in   where they are

together *in country*
for a moment
our standing there

we breathe what air
and closeness to earth
might be

8. Back on the Ship

I stand to shoot the camera
the sea passes
through my reflection

on the sliding doors
the rail triangles my head
and body

I'm a figure
drawn between horizon and ship –
if I'm a watcher   surveyor

diviner of lens-light
aggrandized
in this

I think how earlier the speeding sea-light
on a zodiac   tricked us
to eschew pre-human time

it wasn't easy to look at the island's geology
its high cliffs to the sky
or imagine

the worn down
jagged piece over piece
as remainders

of a long before
or that now our being
is only after all that

9. Venus is Sharply Bright

the land's edge is in ochre
sunset   the sea is folding
like cloth
dark corded
dragging away from the ship

the last small dinghy
is brought back on board

the smell of petrol
a long line of steel   hooks the black
rubber
pulls it high

onto where it's tied
nothing then   except the soft
lighter dark
of the sky against the sea

10. Broome : a Story

I step off the ship
descend from the bus's

high step
I'm landing hard

the driver stops to tells us something
  "the aborigines are not like us"

'not like us' – echoes   I should have said "what is 'us'?"
like my little sister?

called a 'filthy Jew'
at her school"

like me told   "you don't believe in God"
in my school

the driver goes on
"we get a bit wild as kids

then settle down
the aborigines stay in trouble

do nothing
for themselves"

I'm jarred
in my leg too

The bus had let us off in streets
with blank-fronted stores

inside them
glass cases

held pearls satin-set
luminously as the lights over them

The Yawuru began things
for the pearlers

The Yawuru were robbed of their land
Their children kidnapped

then forced to dive
for nothing for themselves

to draw up pearls from depths
through fathoms

of the colourless pushing
against their eyes

and chest-held breaths
legs wide dangling touching nothing

to grab from the sea's floor
in hope   coming up for air

on a surface their head can break through
sometimes without pearls

men beat them back under   with the oars
of boats that took them out

hit their shoulders and heads down again
into the airless muscle of the sea

resisting them   with its moving volumes
shapeless around them

This Planet's Autumn

for Z.P.K.

1.
Autumn light lines a table leg
blisters stars on a table top
sinks
and darkens
It silhouettes trees fronds leaves
yet still shows a ball of gold
radiating
from a corner of the horizon
a building is leaning on —
while the radio's drive-time
music
swings
into the living room long strings
stretching to a fall   a presage of letting go
the day
the day
I have not had long enough   sunniness
brief as dessert on the tongue

2.

Recession into painted space
a willow
streaming fronds
striking further
along the air
the flight of a heron
legs trailing   stretching
wings like fans
waving the air away
like a swimmer
pushing water
in front of the body's
proceeding
the head's all-flowering
water-fountain
the sculptured brimming
of the pool   welling over her
leaves us as art does   set in a new pattern

3.

Our planet around the sun then —
fear
is in understanding
all our astronomic
certainty
is only
about the wear and tear —
earth like us lacks
immortal life
you see in telescopes
microscopes too
their searching after wonders
reveals that space doesn't have
another haven
set in seas
with earth
in emerald green
and rain
or sunniness the same
sweet days
to hold
us breathing
swimming
through

The Travel of Air

It's a wet road
I can hear the rush
on black

on water splashing
on tyres running –
working at night

in the glamour
of car-lights
slowing brightly across the window

no stars   I would inhale stars
space my breath
to be with them

a longer wheel of a car
passes through   goes softly
touching the rain

a faster car throwing the splashes
off
deserts the street

this morning
the traffic of rain has gone
into sun

the difference
as if I had space —
the distance sounds   even

in the clear travel of air
in a small walk
the rush is my breath in the tree that I pass

Wind Darkening the Sea

1.
I was drunk with the sun
at the next wharf the ferry was rocking
docking   banging the pylons
I could see grey splits
in the old
white topped wood
the wind didn't cut out the sun until a cloud
doused it closing off the warm landscape
its waterfront units and mansions

the lovers at the prow of the ferry
looked out   close together   she bareheaded
he wore his hood up — the wind was fierce —
large spots of rain fell
both stayed where everything was wild
wind blew her hair into strands
like black laces tying   untying

We walked over the gangplank
put up an umbrella
this new wharf of fibreglass and steel
slicked off the wet —
we were out in the open

2.

The sea is always darkening and lightening –
on cloudy days
watching from a distance
two ferries
pulling in opposite directions
pushes my eyes to the middle view
where space
stretches the mind's opening
expanding feeling –
when the ferries cross each other   going past a cove
I let my eyes turn with them into the looping inlet
feel the ease of something done
in their pull through heavy water

 I delight in the busyness
of ships on the harbour
or after when looking at the white sea
glittering as the sun breaks through
it's a width to gaze at
no disaster there

Constructing a City

What is it

that a city precinct
makes you look for –
sandstone walls
that seep water onto footpaths

you tread the puddles
glistening on bitumen
walk the slipperiness –
and in the creviced stone

touch the concavities
the convex bulges   irregularly cut –
to stave off
the glassy buildings' shine

so high   your eye
falls
away
from the nothing-you-can reach

the city
steeling
our
senses

thoughts   dense as road-trees'
parallax error
of their going with you
while you're driving past

press you to be
inseparable
from
your pursuits

you look
for a green
interruption

Outside the Botanic Gardens' Iron Fence

easiness of sight and the sense of scents
runs out
on roads and blue and yellow boards
harsh painted ads in case we miss them
walking slowly under trees
or don't want quick prominences
the city brings
the cut glass glitter that clips our eyes
that only the harbour at the end restrains
                                          \

our blinking subsides then
beside sea's rituals

or a fine piece of architecture —
a coloured strut   leaning
earths the fizz

But the House

each room except the kitchen
was a bedroom   the brick laundry   another

cold   the door to the backyard flimsy
all space cramming them to be inner only

thought tightened in awe of what existed
words burst in shouts

words a nuisance   unless few
you could see our faces not finding them in time

in any present   shade and heat make patterns
this present is looking back carefully

perhaps it comes from years
inside the mind   its top spinning

today   the sound of cars on wet roads
each is a spasm   in the rain's rhythm

though it was like velvet   once   on barer roads
cars sidled by   a sweet interruption

memory peels like scraping off paint
from flaking areas

without betterment you're shy   not violent
but the raving echoes

then the newness
a red-topped table   chrome and vinyl chairs

eyes fall from the glare   the slipperiness
shuts them

the backyard is mud
disaffection is sometimes where she gardens

But a Room Now

A table round   dark wood steadied
on a ring of arcing legs
joining the top to the floor
the support like space laced in —
the coloured covered chairs
delight
like the black glazed
vase   its short neck curved around and out
to its full-blown body then back up to the lip
little drops of light shine
on the throat
next   a petalled rim on a blue ceramic vase
running fingers into water
where flower stems rest
these objects pressed into shape then cut
both like plants
the potters thinking   only in a garden —
then the black carvings
one a head with plaited hair
her eyes and mouth discovered
inside the deliberating —
another   a thin figure thinking
hand to chin pausing
the artist
realising

to love all of these   I decide
to place
whatever has been touched
in them

I'm able to touch again
with my eye
or my hand in passing
to pick up
a sculpture in felt
with stitched coloured
markings —
a soft lyre bird head
with two real-bird feathers —
then next the heavy
amber glass
turtle
head and flippers
poking into the light
   nearly yellow

I look then outside the room
at red leaves lit
to pink translucency and green
leaves waving   there nothing is still

Night Light

The silent cyclists
proceeding down the road
at 5 o'clock in the morning

red lit trucks
the first shift of construction workers
arriving
in their quietness
I can't sleep
any longer

That was yesterday
to-night I'm waiting
to sleep
to start sleeping
I look up and down the street
lights on the casino across the water
night lights on the construction site

the dark is pale

Rain in the City

More gloss than light
the harbour-water
is cut through by ferries
slow in sea's thickness

Clarice Beckett streets
the black roads' sheen
and trees' wet dark
hold the rain in a monotone

Archaic

With metronome-ticking head and eyes
a bird
walks on the grass
its noisy-miner mate calls from a tree
in time and beat musically
the first bird's nod is conducting it

a fountain boulder-grey   pours water
from bronze fish mouths
waves of the sea
scroll
in triumph
their majesty

the basin's grey undoes the park's green
the noisy-miner birds
aren't heavy
don't rest on this memorial to history
they're quick and sleight-of-tune
and sight

a tourist or day-off-walker
looking for a photo opportunity
focuses on his lens the shepherdess
stroking her sheep's submissiveness
with head-tilted calm and couch-leaning
poise   she rests a right arm

her queenly stature
and a godly Neptune with his fork
make land-and-sea seizing
look like
child's play

Balcony over Construction Works by the Sea

Iron chairs   shadows scrolled
inked in   on a red metal cabinet

the spangle of the sea's silver
is thrown through glass
onto glass
in the morning

yet from sun to set
indesinent
pendulums of sway and haul
drop scoop and carry
to another place

The Excavations

have sloped banks
like photos of erosion
my imagination smells the dust
the

                    in
smothering   pits   falls
                    ^

from the apartment's height
we can't
think it can't happen

the bright orange   neon green and yellow suits
            of the workers
tidy this thought to a reassurance
the sprinkle of flashing lights everywhere
is it the steady glow of fixed
            high   globes
down there

                    from
                up here

we're comparing them   with the automatic
            switched-on   remotes
                        inside

It Feels like Rain

for IAK

A whirr somewhere
sites with removable barriers
to stare at

her eyes run along
like fingers
over indentations

now they skim over
the rain-stopped stillness
like a fast-flying bird

her suddenness (and again
her start from that)
bring her
to imagining
what could be

The Bridge

the sea's plains pattern the mind
to see durance — from edge to edge

an interval of holding   catches the gap
like a bird pursuing the other side and landing

on the harbour a cruiser's white line
is tripping the water to fold it   in furrows to the shore

the day is sunny   hot   to gather the sea
thickly   ruffled into surf   I'm trying to think of that

away from the suburbs buffed with perfumes
and colours from trees   light green clusters in leaf

their honey light in my eyes —
the bridge greys   against the sea moving   endlessly

connects us to ourselves
to be city-different

as if the shine of glass
(through to an inverted world

or down upon us dazzling)
needs our particular carriage

Water and Light

1. One Unit

I love the stripes of light on walls
or
on the column reaching through the ceiling
supporting the unit above —
light on white indoor paint
falls reflected
is it water or leaves
shaking in the wind
things are getting wilder   the palm tree on the balcony
is blowing about like fire
light is striping the cushions
the carpets   colour jumps about

against the rat-a-tat-tatting
of the jackhammer outside

2. To Think That

whatever thought is   is it like tracing
a pencil around
the moveable episode

noticing the island dweller
throwing food to a flying bird
while water is running over him

3. The Tree Outside

a sea of winds runs the sun
the leaves green into yellow

the tree is a cloud
breaking the light

reflections tremble like water
to the floor

long blinds over windows
are unmoving as the coast

when ships pass

If It Takes a Little Longer

before it's suddenly dark
I can watch the swiftness of a river-cat

or low moving cruiser
to know I'm exactly in the present

though they're walking down by the edge
their senses still stretching for them

a couple   in their casual embrace of time
not yet so silhouetted

by the silvery light
as to become enigmas

their hands-pocketed stroll
is immediate as easy happiness

still the light is even
over everything

only the electric brightness
full-on   on the opposite shore

and a worker's bright orange shirt
standing out on this one

renders the definiteness of evening coming

Our Constant Inner Mobility

after Eric Auerbach

Hauling cranes stall the eye
more than that they are signs
of stilled earth
their dust mist everywhere
the road a drought
life blurs

Once a tree   lush   a bird flying into it
unfolded again
        like any hurried-on thought
before my eyes
had switched
from the bird's first lighting

Driving through then
a sudden brightening
bottle brushes reddened
and a wattle
yellowed through
its massy leaf

Yet now bright glass and traffic lights
a mimicking dazzle
to run with
night and day
as I let
the city be the colour

no earth's plants synthesize

breathing long lines
of unperfumed land

Politics and Anxiety

Vertigo

Sea's giddy wake cranks anxiety to a pitch
that speeding launch the horizon its thrill's edge
a line you're walking parallel to

the foreshore's close the deep water doesn't break
until the lift before the long wave falls

apprehensions you won't avoid —
obsessions last those lock-steps look long
as all degrees of cynicism and unquestioning rise

in the State
or the set of the autocrat's head ranging
stares and smiles

is a kind of power overpowering
is the same
as a-once as well as an-every-time

it will be
you'll feel the height — the deepening
in the oscillating sea's
fall

The News (Redacted)

Under the trees
the filtering of noise and light
hides the buildings

here no trees but the tall shine of glass and a glaze on floors
thoughts shallow in the mirrors   subsume adversaries
in the flickering   in the dazzle   of whatever works

as if to resolve differences coming up in conversation
'you know'   they say   after reading the spin
of the news   *copy that —*

their satisfaction   whatever's left
of understanding   empty as the chairs outside
that sit and wait for café-goers in the wind
and shade of a cold day

The News (2)

as streets
turn like rivers and cross
under tunnelled hills

as caves
open in cliffs the sea explodes
against

as more roads widen
pushing trees and plants
away

we have the news

They

experiment
with
games
strategy
on a
theologically
centred
tribal
society's
codes
of
retribution

murdering
civilians

Ministers and Members of Parliament or "Bliss"

after Ange Mlinko

They turn black circles with long necks
their red beaks into feathered backs
swans draw rings around all watching
the cynosure of eyes   their stretch
and bend   their float on this park lake
we find proportion everywhere
in the green beside them   to see this
when stopping   after beginning to go
stooping to smell one more rose

is to notice tourists who look too   who remind us
of something else   it's a flick of the eye
beginning to shut   it's abrupt
we know already it's not what we want   of the others
of the hurt who flee to us   whom we flee from

dear ministers and members of Parliament
the hurt who flee to us   we flee from them

where to start not seeing them   not to hear what they're calling
but to detain   to keep waiting   to make late
to be heard   to imprison past the time
allowed by law   except where the law is the one that's made
for keeping people who are seeking
our attention   not to get it   help or hope

And *in extremis* to bring on extremes
to stop the cries to disguise all calls

when lives are at their stopping points
this reasoning
what's the point in knowing their cries
out of earshot   we can imagine still
we sent troops didn't we   to kill?   here are children
men and women running
ministers and members of parliament   you can see them
through your cunning
and your eyes

Dog Whistle

'He whistles his hounds to stay close.'
  – Paul Celan, *Death Fugue*

The prancing Dalmatian in the park
entering
on the first warm Spring day
then the poodle and the bitzer

See the high-stepping poodle
alternate in poise and pose
within the trees' shadows

Ezra – "how am I seen?"

                          the poet reflecting on the mirror –
                          a "middle-class-conformist"
                          error
                          fills him so late
                          with "avant-gardist" shame

                          he is Mussolini's fan
                          the poet so proper
                          unbeautiful
hates
madly
out of date
his words

now Donald too
"do I look like a dope?"
"I'll look stupid"

                              will show-biz let him off
                              for the un-cool deal?

                              his misgiving is fake
                              no starry vision

he's not furious

till caught phoning bribes

and he's played in a trial

no whistles to his base
will bring him better looks

the leaves and light
brightly green and yellow
and the shadows
under them on grass

what tunes it listens to
a dog its heard voices scanning

Border Crossing

The rooves they were flying over –
like a lead balloon, she said –
her mood
not thinking of flying

we are not now going through
security
note the head
turning is it

palm trees in blue shadow
the sea folds to the land's circumference
hills travel

new road-kill now   brown furry or smashed red

kangaroos   in warning signs
just "jump" across

Infinite Jest

The sea was the colour
of the underside of leaves
in a banksia tree

the sound of words
the stutter of not saying
yet ticking out time

going back to what was

the sea is lined another way now
is the sky's transparency
yet so full

the land dipping into it
presses all the hue-less
water into blue

concentration's
in the words
meaning   you're joking

the politician
who cannot
get away with that

we're all thinking

as the light in stripes
piles
on the silly sea

Heights like Little Cartoons

of a fear
of falling
from the hotel on the hill
you must slide or climb

see verticals for the fun
of looking up or down –
evenness
has the same lines

in bars on windows
inside and out
    the look-out is marking
high walls

see precipices
as floorless depths'
diminishments

Dissonance

Voices too known
yours and mine in anxious
placating

crossing like this
to get on   to go on
without bumping

collisions now
in this sort of traffic
not fun

dodging the sound
is almost making me
deaf

I mustn't hear you
the high fidelity's
on

Numb

Of art Gerhardt Richter said

so it's all evasive action in a way

In France   Richter's paintings —
one is a photograph he's tampered with
blurring what is fixed

he's caressing or undoing the image
of his aunt Marianne — an older child
who shyly holds him (a baby)

Marianne "euthanized"   gassed   for being slow
 (a Nazi "correction")
Richter's brush

breaks up the photo
paints it out of focus
what is familial   quietly

quivers in art
time stalls
redress in action

the only likeness
"*That which has happened*"
not to be forgotten

~

painting his uncle Rudi too
soldier shining
smiling in uniform – killed at the war's start –

Richter will say "a young and very stupid man" –
the dragged paint for the warrior sprawl
Rudi overcome by overcoat small youthful

pervasive the art
showing
what was hidden to the child

the pieces now
in the artist's embrace –
the killers   "purer Aryans"   than Marianne

Nazi eugenics
to procure the "prized"
the fatherland's favourites   the murderers

their unflinching stroke
never erased
makes a fool of Rudi

grief
the artists' brief

25th April 2013

Did you see the photograph in today's *Herald*
Six soldiers   trouser pockets bulging
like muscles on their thighs
each with a gun sliding over camouflage patterns
to catch the shadows of grass and trees

would you say like Plath as she mocks
'Every woman adores a fascist/ The boot
in the face, the brute/Brute heart of a brute…'
but look
at their faces   to the front at their eyes
staring   round with pupils' big dots   others squinting
or open   even vague   at beck   waiting for orders
or for the camera to go away

The headline says they're 'coming home…the 9/11 generation'
Anzac Day

it seems
not   'never again'
but always
new growing
just harvest them
the way they hold
themselves and the gun

View

Buffoons rule
loony tunes
become them
and us? inured to nonsense (almost)
the noise derisible still
listen to prime ministers and presidents
joke in their charnel house

Some too stretched to notice

unlucky last to speak   traduced
look at what's on now
it's in the news

The Insect Feeling

when spotlights pick up
the unexpected identity
edged out of you
your disappearance into others
your outer limbs touching
and slipping down the stem
of the flower you hide behind
the showy orchid's velvet
centre
its red   yellow
and pink skirt   flares
as you fall   noting
your invisibility's
an intact
acceptance
though you're dizzy with seeing
past the flower
to the one holding it
the other-eyed
clearness   that can't see you

Titian and the Male Gaze

Her bow hand drawn
twists a curve in Acteon's fall
Diana in a wine-coloured gown
right-armed   breast bared
Acteon slopes
antlered now   feet deep in water
in deep   in shadows
the hounds in their streaming together
see doe eyes   prey
as Acteon
noses into toppling air

he's leaning over
bent-back front
can't rise like a stag
staggers too human
no quick in him   not enough for flight
his frightened head is passive-eyed

to Titian's men Acteon's
unmanned and animalised
Diana high goddess
paradox perhaps
unknowable
"wilder than a man"
if a woman

Child

The deep eyed pull of grief
you know it
you smile
wanting to hope

you show that
and ask
small questions
you think they haven't

except you are frightened
with them
worse will come
it's a thought

your brain
folds in
young
yet you cannot rest on

you see
you have
like any bridge

from there
to here to there

that brush of other life

Epilogue

That Past

then when
I felt I didn't know
still excitement
was quick

but now this
except I should think
in colour and sound
like the movies
understanding is on our watch

Acknowledgements

Previously published poems in *But Now*:
"The Unsafe World" – Australian Poetry Anthology Vol 4–1 2014
"Ministers and Members of Parliament" –Writing to the Wire 2016
"The Travel of Air" (slightly different version) – This Gift this Poem 2021

I thank my partner Max Deutscher for his love and support. My children, Zoe, Alex, Matthew and Isabel Karpin and their children, gave me their appreciation and were an inspiration also my sisters Sylvia Bennet and Valda Lynch.

I also thank my fellow poets in Youngstreet workshop and the poets in Judy Beveridge's 'master' (I call it) class for their support and friendship.

www.ingramcontent.com/pod-product-compliance
Lightning Source LLC
Chambersburg PA
CBHW020906100426
42737CB00044B/527